The LAST FIREHAWK

The Ember Stone

by
Katrina Charman
illustrated by
Jeremy Norton

BRANCHES™
SCHOLASTIC INC.

The LAST FIREHAWK

Read All the Books

1

2

3

More books
coming soon!

Table of Contents

Introduction 1

Map 2

Chapter 1: Training Time 4

Chapter 2: An Important Discovery 11

Chapter 3: The Golden Egg 18

Chapter 4: Run! 22

Chapter 5: Rising from the Ashes 26

Chapter 6: Grey's Tale 30

Chapter 7: Tiger Bat Attack! 37

Chapter 8: Blaze 43

Chapter 9: Adventure Calls! 48

Chapter 10: Fire Island 52

Chapter 11: Over the Waves 59

Chapter 12: Not Alone 63

Chapter 13: Spies? 67

Chapter 14: Into Danger 74

Chapter 15: The Ember Stone 80

Chapter 16: Return of the Firehawk 86

For Maddie, Piper, and Riley. —KC
Thank you to my parents, who showed me the value of art. —JN

Library of Congress Cataloging-in-Publication Data

Names: Charman, Katrina, author. Title: The ember stone / by Katrina Charman; Description: First edition. New York, NY : Branches/Scholastic Inc., 2017. Series: The last firehawk ; 1 | Summary: Perodia is threatened by Thorn, a powerful vulture, who is using magic to spread a terrible darkness—but when a young owl named Tag, and his best friend, the squirrel Skyla, rescue a golden egg from Thorn's Tiger bats they may have found the key to Perodia's salvation: the last firehawk, guardian of the ember stone.

Subjects: LCSH: Owls—Juvenile fiction. | Squirrels—Juvenile fiction. | Animals, Mythical—Juvenile fiction. | Magic—Juvenile fiction. |. Rescues—Juvenile fiction. | Adventure stories. |CYAC: Owls—Fiction. | Squirrels—Fiction. |. Animals, Mythical—Fiction. | Fantasy. | GSAFD: Adventure fiction. | LCGFT: Action and adventure fiction.]
Classification: LCC PZ7.1.C495 Em 2016 | DDC [Fic]—dc23 LC record available at https://lccn.loc.gov/2016054929

ISBN: 978-93-5275-236-2

First edition, October 2017
Edited by Katie Carella
Book design by Jessica Meltzer
This reprint edition February 2026
Printed in India at Shivam Offset Press, New Delhi

INTRODUCTION

In the enchanted land of Perodia, lies Valor Wood—a forest filled with magic and light. There, a wise old owl named Grey leads the Owls of Valor. These brave warriors protect the many creatures of the wood. But a darkness is spreading across Perodia, and the forest's magic and light are fading away . . .

A powerful old vulture called Thorn controls The Shadow—a dark magic. He is using it to destroy Perodia and the homes of all who live there. Rivers are drying up. Trees are losing their leaves. Thorn will not stop until Perodia is destroyed.

Tag, a small barn owl, dreams of becoming an Owl of Valor. He wants to protect his forest. He wants to fight Thorn and his army of spies. But Tag needs more than just courage and bravery. Only the brightest magic can beat the darkness.

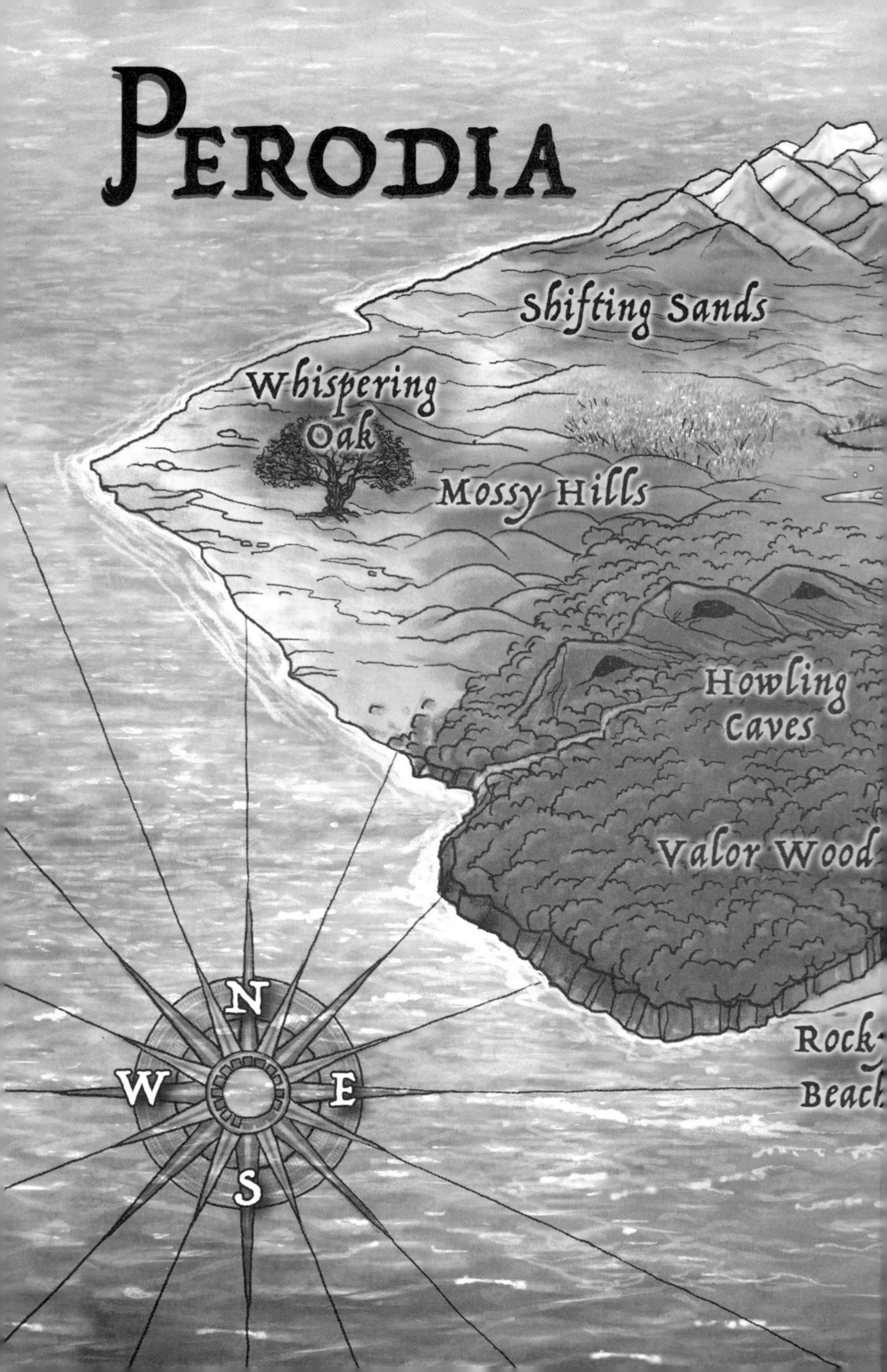

PERODIA
Shifting Sands
Whispering Oak
Mossy Hills
Howling Caves
Valor Wood
Rock-
Beach
N
W
E
S

Crystal Caverns
Jagged Mountains
Bubbling Bog
Lullaby Lake
The Shadowlands
Blue Bay
Fire Island

TRAINING TIME

TA-RAAAA! A horn sounded through Valor Wood.

Tag watched as owls of all sizes swooped down from the trees.

Training time! Tag thought, excitement bubbling in his tummy.

He hopped off his branch to join a group of young owls.

Maximus, the captain of the Owls of Valor, stood in the center of camp.

"You are all here to learn how to fight," Maximus announced. "As you know, our magical forest is in danger. Only the bravest warriors can protect it. And only the bravest warriors will become Owls of Valor."

Tag puffed up his chest. He wanted to become an Owl of Valor more than anything.

"Choose your weapons!" Maximus yelled. His voice had one setting: Very Loud.

The weapons were lined up. Tag stood beside a bow and arrow—too tall. Next, he lifted a sword—too heavy. He picked up a shiny dagger—it was just right.

Tag chose the smallest shield—it was as big as he was!

I may be small now, but I won't give up until I'm strong enough to hold the biggest shield, Tag thought.

All day, Maximus showed the young owls how to duck and dive. Tag attacked tree trunks with the dagger. His wings got weaker as he struggled to hold the heavy shield.

SCREE-EEE! Suddenly, Grey flew down to land beside Maximus. His bright yellow eyes sparkled with magic.

The owls gathered around in silence, waiting for their leader to speak.

"All animals are now forbidden to go near the Howling Caves!" Grey said.

Tag raised his shaky wing. "But . . . why?" he asked. The caves were his favorite place to explore.

"The caves are too dangerous," Grey warned. He waved a wing and an image appeared beside his head.

Tiger bats! thought Tag.

The tiger bats' huge, orange eyes glowed. Their long, sharp beaks snapped at the air.

"Thorn's army of tiger bats has been seen near the caves," Grey said. He waved his wing again and a dark cloud appeared. In its center was the tiger bats' master, Thorn.

Tag shivered. The old and powerful vulture would stop at nothing to destroy Valor Wood.

Grey's magical cloud disappeared. He stretched out his huge wings and flew off.

"Back to training!" Maximus yelled. "Find a partner!"

The owls quickly paired up, leaving a large, brown owl named Bod for Tag to work with. Tag held up his shield and stood as tall as he could while Bod looked him up and down.

The shield slipped from Tag's tired wing. It clattered to the ground.

Bod laughed. "You'll never be an Owl of Valor! You can't even hold a shield!"

Tag felt his face burn.

They practiced until Tag could barely hold his dagger.

"That's enough for today!" Maximus shouted.

Tag looked at Bod. *I may not be big and strong,* Tag thought, *but I am* brave *enough to be an Owl of Valor. I'll find a way to prove it!*

CHAPTER 2

AN IMPORTANT DISCOVERY

Tag stomped through the woods on his way home.

He heard a rustle nearby. Someone . . . or some*thing* was watching. Tag picked up a stick. Footsteps scritched and scratched through the dry leaves.

Closer. Closer. Until . . .

"Gotcha!"

"Ahhh!" Tag yelled.

A small gray squirrel fell to the ground laughing.

"Scaredy owl!"

"Skyla! That's not funny!" Tag said. "I almost hit you."

"That twig wouldn't hurt me," his best friend replied. "I thought you were a brave warrior?"

"I am," Tag said. "One day, I'm going to be an Owl of Valor and save the wood from the evil—"

Skyla jumped up and put her paw over Tag's beak. "Don't say his name!"

“I’m not afraid of Thorn,” Tag mumbled.

Skyla’s eyes went wide. “You should be.”

Tag looked at the river. It used to be full of clear blue water. Now it was dry—because of Thorn.

He walked on, kicking at the dusty ground.

“I know what will cheer you up!” Skyla tapped Tag on the wing. “You’re it!”

“No fair!” Tag chased after her. “I can’t run as fast as you.”

But I can fly! Tag took off, gliding through the trees.

After a few minutes, he called, "Skyla! Where are you?"

"I'm here!" Skyla giggled.

Tag landed beside her and looked around. They had gone farther than he'd thought. "Oh no," Tag groaned. "We are at the Howling Caves! Grey told us to stay away."

"Let's get out of here!" Skyla said, looking at the three creepy caves.

There was a sudden whisper on the wind. A black cloud covered the sun so that it was almost as dark as night.

"The Shadow!" Skyla grabbed her slingshot.

"It's probably just a storm," Tag said. He flapped closer to the largest cave.

"Don't go in there!" Skyla warned.

This could be my chance to prove how brave I am, Tag thought.

The cave looked like a mouth open wide, ready to gobble them up. The wind blew harder and howled around them.

No wonder these are called the Howling Caves, Tag thought.

"Don't worry, Skyla," Tag said. "Tiger bats only come out at night."

"Who said anything about tiger bats?" Skyla asked.

"Um . . . Grey did," Tag said. He pointed to the dark sky. "Come on! We need somewhere to shelter from the storm."

Tag peered into the deep, dark cave. A red light glowed. "What's that?" He hopped inside, heading toward the light.

"I don't like this," Skyla said, loading her slingshot. "But someone has to make sure you don't get eaten!"

Tag smiled to show he wasn't scared, but his feathers were shaking.

The friends walked toward the glowing light. The cold cave felt warmer as they neared it.

"What is that?" Skyla asked.

Tag hopped closer for a better look. He blinked. "It's . . . a golden egg."

The biggest, brightest egg Tag had ever seen.

CHAPTER 3

THE GOLDEN EGG

Tag stared at the huge, glowing egg. "I've never seen an egg this big before!"

"I've never seen a *golden* egg before," Skyla said. "What do you think it is?"

"I don't know," Tag said. "But I bet the tiger bats stole it. We have to get it out of here."

"Wait!" Skyla cried. "It could *be* a tiger bat!"

Tag laughed. "Bats don't lay eggs, silly."

"Tiger bats are not normal bats," Skyla said. "Anyway, how are we going to move it?"

Tag frowned. The egg was bigger than both of them. "Maybe we could roll it?"

He pressed a wing against the egg.

"Ow! It's hot!" Tag shook his sizzling feathers.

"Stay here. I have an idea!" Skyla scurried out of the cave. Outside, the sky had cleared and the sun was bright again.

"See? It was just a passing storm," Tag told the egg.

Skyla returned with armfuls of leaves and sticks.

"I'll make a cart." Her quick fingers twisted the leaves and sticks together. Soon, the cart was finished.

Together, Tag and Skyla nudged the egg onto the cart.

"Poor egg, all alone in this creepy cave," Tag said.

Skyla looked back at Tag. She gasped and pointed a shaky finger. "Um, Tag . . . I don't think it *was* alone . . ."

Tag turned. A pair of big, bright eyes stared at him. Another pair slowly opened. Then another and another—until hundreds of beady, orange eyes glared back.

CHAPTER 4

RUN!

The tiger bats' bright orange eyes watched from the darkness.

"Tiger bats!" yelled Tag. "Grey was right!"

"And we've woken them up!" Skyla cried.

Tag and Skyla pushed and pulled at the cart. It didn't move.

"Hurry!" Tag said.

"The egg is too heavy!" Skyla huffed.

Tag gave a big push. The egg wobbled, then—**THUNK!** It fell off the cart.

I hope it's not cracked, thought Tag.

The tiger bats' wings scraped the walls. One landed close by with a **THUD!**

The egg started to roll out of the cave and down the hill.

"Follow that egg!" Tag yelled.

The friends raced behind the egg as the tiger bats flew out of the cave, zooming back and forth. **SQUAWK!**

"Good thing tiger bats can't see well in daylight!" Skyla puffed. "We should be able to lose them out here!"

Tag's heart pounded. Blasts of air from the tiger bats' giant orange-and-black striped wings pushed him on.

The egg picked up speed as it rolled downhill.

It banged into an old fallen tree and stopped.

"We have to hide!" Skyla said. "Before the bats see us!"

Tag looked at the fallen tree. "Quick—let's hide in here!"

He used a stick to shove the egg into the hollow trunk. Then he and Skyla crawled in behind it.

CLACK, CLACK, CLACK. Tag and Skyla held their breath as the tiger bats' beaks snapped above them.

After a while, it was quiet.

"That was close," Skyla said.

"I know," Tag sighed. Then he grinned. "But we did it—we saved the egg!"

The sun was setting. They were too tired to move the egg, so the friends rested in a nearby tree.

"I'll keep watch," Tag said with a yawn.

But soon, they both fell fast asleep.

CHAPTER 5

RISING FROM THE ASHES

WAAA-RAAA! An alarm sounded.

Tag woke with a start. The moon was high in the sky. Below, something flickered brightly.

"Fire!" he yelled.

Black smoke filled the air. "The egg!" Skyla cried.

Flames rose from the old fallen tree.

Tag gasped. "The egg was *hot*—it must have set the tree on fire!"

The friends raced down from their branch. They scooped up water to pour onto the flames.

Finally, all that was left was a smoky pile of ashes. Pieces of golden eggshell glittered among the ashes.

"The egg is destroyed!" Tag cried. "We're going to be in *such* big trouble. Now we went into the Howling Caves and woke the tiger bats for nothing! And we started a fire!"

Skyla patted Tag on the back. "At least we put out the fire before it spread."

Something snuffled beside them.

"Look!" Tag said.

Covered in ash, blinking its big, blue eyes, was a very large baby bird.

"ACHOO!" The bird sneezed, sending up a cloud of ash. Her beautiful feathers were gold, red, and orange. They sparkled brightly, lighting the dark wood.

Skyla stared. "A firehawk!"

Tag shook his head. "But . . . there's no such thing as a firehawk."

CHAPTER 6

GREY'S TALE

The baby bird stretched her wings.

"I'm Tag," Tag told the bird. "This is Skyla. She thinks you're a firehawk."

Skyla put her paws on her hips. "She *is* a firehawk. My grandma told me they had bright, sparkling feathers." She pointed to the bird's glittering wings.

SCREE-EEE! A loud screech echoed through the wood. Grey appeared as if from nowhere. He did not look happy.

"It wasn't our fault," Tag started, "not *exactly* . . ."

Then Grey saw the baby bird.

"What do we have here?" Grey smiled at the bird. "I didn't think I'd ever see a firehawk again . . ."

"I told you, Tag!" said Skyla.

"She really *is* a firehawk?" Tag asked.

"Yes," said Grey. "You have made an important discovery. I thought the firehawks were all gone."

"What happened to them?" Tag asked.

"The firehawks were magical birds who protected the Ember Stone—a stone that holds powerful magic within it," Grey explained. "They did everything in their power to stop Thorn from finding the stone. But one day, the firehawks vanished."

Skyla gasped. "That's terrible!"

"Could the Ember Stone stop Thorn and The Shadow?" asked Tag.

Grey stroked his chin. "Maybe. The stone's magic could be even stronger than Thorn's dark magic. But Thorn is moving fast. Trees are dying. The wood's good magic is fading. Can you feel it?"

Tag and Skyla nodded. Valor Wood was changing. Flowers no longer bloomed. Rivers were dry. It wouldn't be long before Thorn destroyed everything.

"Where is the stone now?" Skyla asked.

"I do not know, but I do know that Thorn never found it. If he had, he would have already used it to destroy Perodia," Grey replied. "The firehawks lived on Fire Island, so the stone might still be there—hidden somewhere only a firehawk can find it."

Grey looked at the baby bird. "Where did you find her egg?"

Tag took a deep breath. Owls of Valor were brave and true. He had to tell the truth.

"At the Howling Caves," Tag replied. "We thought Thorn and his tiger bats had stolen the egg, so we tried to save it."

"That was very brave," Grey said. "But I forbid anyone to go near those caves."

"I'm sorry," Tag said, secretly pleased that Grey had called him brave.

"We didn't mean to start a fire," Skyla added.

"The fire was not your fault," Grey told them. "Firehawks hatch in flame."

TA-RAAAA! A horn sounded in the distance.

"We're under attack!" Grey shouted. "I must gather the Owls of Valor."

"Can I come?" Tag asked.

Grey held up a wing. "You two stay with the firehawk."

Skyla nodded. "We'll keep her safe."

"But I can fight!" Tag cried.

Grey shook his head. "There are more ways than one to protect our forest, Tag. It is not always the biggest or strongest owls who become Owls of Valor. Keep the firehawk safe—and hidden. There is only one reason Thorn would have a firehawk egg: He wanted this firehawk to lead him to the Ember Stone. We can't let Thorn find her."

Grey disappeared into the trees, as a dark cloud filled the sky.

CHAPTER 7

TIGER BAT ATTACK!

The Owls of Valor flew overhead in their shining armor.

"Come on!" Skyla said, pulling at Tag's wing. "We have to hide the firehawk."

Tag and Skyla tried to lift the baby bird.

Tag groaned. "She's . . . too . . . heavy!"

Hundreds of tiger bats circled above. Their orange eyes glowed in the darkness.

Skyla loaded her slingshot. "Thorn's army is coming for the firehawk!"

"We can't let them find her!" Tag said, grabbing a heavy stick.

Tag leaned in to speak to the trembling baby bird. "Can you fly?" he asked.

The firehawk gave a small peep.

Tag moved his wings up and down slowly so as not to scare her. "Can you do this?" Tag wasn't sure firehawks *could* fly.

The baby bird ruffled her feathers, but stayed on the ground.

"I guess not," said Skyla.

Tag sighed. "Let's hide in the grove—it's close by. The thick bushes should help hide her bright feathers."

Tag and Skyla hurried through the trees. The firehawk wobbled on unsteady legs as they led her into the grove.

The baby bird peeped, flapping her wings.

"Stay quiet," Tag whispered.

Suddenly—**SQUAWK!** A tiger bat dived down.

Skyla fired a pinecone at its head. "Stay back!" she shouted, hitting it between the eyes.

The tiger bat flew dizzily away.

Tag held the stick tightly.

A tiger bat crashed through the trees, then another. Their sharp beaks snapped at Tag and Skyla. **CLACK, CLACK, CLACK.**

Skyla darted up a tree to shoot acorns. She moved so fast she was a blur.

I have to lead them away from the firehawk! Tag thought. He rushed to the other side of the grove.

The larger tiger bat followed. Tag lifted the stick and jabbed it at the tiger bat.

SQUAWK! SQUAWK!

"He's calling the others, Skyla!" Tag yelled. "Get ready!"

Skyla shot acorns from her branch. But each time she hit one bat, another landed nearby.

Tag swung the heavy stick with trembling wings. He couldn't hold it much longer.

"There are too many!" Skyla cried.

Thorn's army moved in.

Tag was surrounded. He took a step backward. Then—

SKRAAA!

The tiger bats spun around. They watched as the firehawk ran out from the bushes.

"SKRAAA!" she called, her glowing wings held high.

There was a flash of light and heat. Tag covered his eyes. He heard the whoosh of many wings, then all was quiet.

When he looked again, the tiger bats were gone. And so was the dark cloud.

BLAZE

Skyla scurried down from her tree. "Where did Thorn's army go?"

Tag blinked. "The firehawk scared them away!"

The baby bird gave a happy little peep. Her gold and red feathers ruffled in the breeze.

"That was amazing!" Tag said to the firehawk. "Hey, we should name you . . . How about Blaze?"

"I like it!" Skyla grinned.

Blaze gave another peep.

"Now let's find Grey," Tag said.

Tag, Skyla, and Blaze hurried through the woods. They hid as best they could in case Thorn's spies were still close by.

Tag was glad to see there was not much damage in camp. A few nests had been destroyed, and the armor hut had been knocked over. But that was it.

Tag led his friends to Grey's tree.

SCREE-EEE! Grey landed beside them.

"I've been looking for you," Grey said, opening the door. "Quickly, bring your new friend inside."

"Her name is Blaze," Tag said.

Grey smiled. "It suits you," he told Blaze.

Tag had never been inside Grey's nest before. Wooden steps led to the very top of the tree, opening into a room filled with books.

"What happened?" Grey asked.

"Thorn's army found us," Tag said. "We tried to fight, but they surrounded us, then Blaze screeched."

"She saved us," Skyla added. "Thorn's army disappeared!"

"The cry of the firehawk," Grey said. "It must have scared them away."

"They were looking for her. Weren't they?" Tag asked.

"Yes, I was afraid of this," Grey said. "Thorn won't give up now that he knows Blaze has hatched. We must find the Ember Stone before Thorn does. We will need it in order to defeat him. It may be our only weapon against his dark magic."

"You should call the Owls of Valor right away," Tag said. "We need that stone!"

Grey put a wing on Tag's shoulder. "This is not a job for the Owls of Valor," he said. "Only this firehawk—along with you and Skyla—can find the stone."

ADVENTURE CALLS!

Tag looked at Blaze. Then he turned back to Grey. “Do you really think a barn owl, a squirrel, and a baby bird can battle Thorn?”

“We need the Ember Stone, Tag,” Grey said. “Blaze already trusts you and Skyla. And it is Blaze who will find the stone.”

Tag knew what he had to do. "We'll do it," he said. "Skyla, Blaze, and me. We will go to Fire Island and find the stone."

Grey smiled. Then he quickly searched through some papers on his desk. He pulled out a rolled-up piece of paper, and gave it to Tag. "This will show you the way."

Tag tucked it beneath his wing.

Grey opened a large cabinet filled with weapons. He turned, holding up two sets of armor. One for Tag, made of silver. One for Skyla in bronze. "I had these made for you."

Tag tried his on. It fit perfectly. “How did you know we would need armor?”

“I am very old.” Grey smiled. “There is not much that I do not know.” He handed Tag a golden dagger. It felt lighter than a feather.

“Wow!” Tag said. “This blade is sharper than a tiger bat’s beak!”

“This is for you, Skyla.” Grey gave Skyla a slingshot made from the finest wood.

She grinned. “I’ll be able to shoot even faster now!”

"What about Blaze?" Tag asked.

"Her feathers are stronger than any armor," Grey said. "And you've seen how fearsome her cry is."

Tag and Skyla nodded.

"Sleep here tonight," Grey continued. "I'll be on the lookout for Thorn's spies, so I won't see you off. Keep your weapons close at all times. And remember: Thorn could attack at any moment. Good luck." Grey flew away into the night.

Tag gripped his dagger. He felt a shiver of excitement as he looked at Skyla and Blaze. "Tomorrow, we head for Fire Island," Tag said. "Where no owl—or squirrel—has gone before!"

FIRE ISLAND

The next morning, Tag readied their supplies. He packed nuts, berries, and his favorite snack—worms. He also packed a large water pouch.

"Ready?" Skyla asked, wearing her new armor.

Tag grinned. "Ready!"

They woke up a sleepy Blaze, and set off along the winding path through Valor Wood. Tag smiled as he glided through the trees. He was ready for adventure.

They traveled for hours, the cool breeze at their backs. Suddenly—

"Ow!" Skyla cried, hopping up and down. "Something bit me!"

Tag landed and looked at the ground. *Why is this soil red and not brown?*

Blaze stomped her feet.

"The ground is moving!" Skyla cried.

Tag took a closer look. "The ground isn't moving—it's covered in prickle ants!"

Tiny red ants covered the soil. Their eyes were bright orange—just like the tiger bats.

"Thorn's spies!" Tag said.

"They're climbing all over me!" cried Skyla.

The three friends hopped along, trying to escape. But the prickle ants crawled up their legs, biting and stinging.

"We'll have to jump in the water to wash them off!" Tag shouted, as they reached a fast-flowing stream.

"I can't swim!" Skyla cried.

"I can't either," Tag said. "But it's not deep."

Tag led Skyla and Blaze into the cool water.

They all climbed out as fast as they could.

"It worked!" Tag said, shaking water from his feathers.

Skyla squeezed water out of her tail. "Yes, but if the ants found us, that means Thorn knows where we are."

Tag shivered. He didn't like feeling that Thorn was so close by.

"You're right. We need to hurry." Tag pulled out Grey's paper. "Grey said this would show us the way—maybe it's a map?"

"I don't understand," Skyla said, looking over Tag's shoulder. "It's blank."

"Look!" Tag gasped as a small dot appeared on the paper. It grew bigger as he watched. There were shapes of land and water, and names of places he had never heard of. "It *is* a map!"

Blaze tapped the map with her beak. She hopped toward a path.

"I think Blaze wants us to go that way," Tag said.

The friends followed the path for hours. Finally, they reached the edge of the forest and looked out over a wide sea. Far in the distance was an island. It looked like a mountain rising from the sea.

"Is that it?" Skyla asked, peering across the dark, choppy water.

Tag nodded. "Fire Island."

CHAPTER 11

OVER THE WAVES

Skyla looked out across the waves. "Fire Island seems *very* far away," she said. "How do we get to it?"

Tag frowned. He was too tired to fly such a long way. Skyla and Blaze couldn't fly at all. "I'm not sure . . . But we've come so far!" he said. "There must be a way across the water."

"PEEP!" Blaze called, peering over a rock at the water's edge.

"What is it?" Tag asked as he and Skyla hurried over.

A large, wrinkled turtle smiled up at them.

"Hullo. I'm Thaddeus." The turtle spoke very s-l-o-w-l-y.

Then Thaddeus saw Blaze. "A firehawk! I haven't seen a firehawk for a very long time." He sighed. "There used to be lots of them. But not anymore."

"Where did they go?" Skyla asked.

"I do not know," said Thaddeus. "Many years ago, there was a big storm. The biggest I have ever seen. The sky grew *so* dark that even the firehawks' bright feathers were hidden. There was a great battle between the firehawks and an old and powerful vulture."

"Thorn!" Tag said.

Thaddeus nodded. "After the storm, the firehawks were never seen again." He turned to Blaze. "Until now."

Tag pointed to Fire Island. "We need to get over there. Can you help us?"

Thaddeus smiled. "I'd be happy to help a firehawk and her friends."

The three friends climbed onto Thaddeus's shell. They held tightly on to one another as Thaddeus sailed over the waves.

NOT ALONE

The sun was setting as they reached the beach.

"Thanks, Thaddeus," said Tag.

"Call when you need me," said the old turtle as he shuffled away.

"What now?" Skyla asked.

"Let's explore the island," said Tag.

Tag sniffed. A smoky smell filled the air. He wiped a wing across his face. He missed the cool shade of Valor Wood. "Fire Island is really hot! And quiet—where are all the animals?"

"I bet Thorn scared them away," Skyla said.

"Thorn's darkness is spreading," Tag said. The trunks of some nearby palm trees were gray and crumbling.

"Peep!" Blaze prodded Skyla.

Skyla looked up at the trees. "The fruit is all rotten!" Black bananas and mangoes hung from the branches.

"I'm glad we packed our own food," said Tag.

"Let's eat," said Skyla. "I'm starving!"

Tag opened the sack. He gulped down some worms and handed Skyla and Blaze some nuts to eat. "Where are the berries?"

Skyla frowned as she peered inside. "They're all gone. And so is the map!"

Blaze peeped, flapping her bright wings.

"What is it?" Tag asked.

Skyla grabbed her slingshot. "Tiger bats?"

Tag pulled out his dagger. "I'll take a look." He flapped up into the long, gray palm leaves. The branches creaked.

Two small spider monkeys stared back at him. They had brown fur and long bushy tails. Their white faces were covered in berry juice.

One of them held up the special map that Grey had given Tag.

"Hey! That's ours!" Tag shouted.

The monkeys giggled.

"Give that back!" Skyla called up to them.

The monkeys leaped to another tree, then scurried away from the beach. Tag, Skyla, and Blaze raced up the rocky mountainside after them—toward the very top of Fire Island . . .

CHAPTER 13

SPIES?

The spider monkeys hurried up the mountain. Tag, Skyla, and Blaze followed.

The higher they climbed, the smokier the air became. When they reached the top, Tag saw why . . .

"Fire Island is a volcano?!" he cried.

"That must be why it's called Fire Island," said Skyla. Her tail twitched. "It's not going to blow, is it?"

Tag paused. "I hope not!"

"Do you think the monkeys are Thorn's spies?" Skyla whispered as they continued to chase them.

Tag shook his head. "I don't think so. They don't have orange eyes."

All of a sudden, Blaze peeped and hopped back and forth. The monkeys had stopped to catch their breath.

"Hey!" Skyla called. She shot a stone into the trees above. The monkeys jumped. They dropped the map as they scurried away.

Skyla picked it up. Beside it was a long, golden feather. "Look at this," she said, holding up the feather.

"That looks like one of Blaze's feathers, but bigger," Tag said. *Maybe there are firehawks on the island after all?*

Tag put the feather into his sack as Blaze peeped behind him.

Tag and Skyla turned around to see a large, red rock painted with bright, colorful birds—birds that looked just like Blaze.

Tag stepped up to the rock. Some of it was covered in black sand. He brushed it away with his wing. "Firehawks!" Tag said. "It looks like these pictures tell a story."

There were four paintings. The first showed so many firehawks that Tag couldn't count them. A large firehawk with golden feathers on his head stood in the middle. *He must be their leader,* Tag thought. The leader held a large purple stone.

"The Ember Stone!" Skyla whispered.

She pointed to the next painting. It showed the Ember Stone glowing purple.

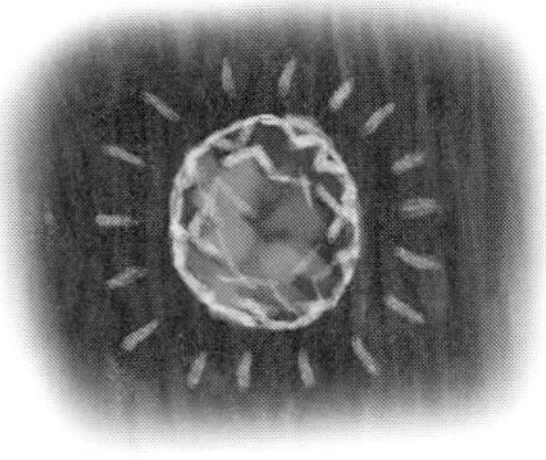

Tag moved over to the third painting. He tried to brush the sand away, but it was stuck. "I wish we could see this picture."

The fourth painting showed Thorn, surrounded by a dark swirly cloud.

"Thorn!" Tag shuddered. Even in the painting, Thorn—and The Shadow—looked scary.

"We need to find that stone," Skyla said.

"Where should we look?" Tag said. "The paintings show the stone. But there are no clues about where it is hidden."

"We'll just have to search the whole island," said Skyla.

The friends searched all day. Tag looked behind every rock.

Skyla climbed every tree.

Even Blaze helped, digging holes with her feet.

"Maybe the Ember Stone is not here after all," Skyla grumbled. "We've looked everywhere."

Blaze rested her head on Skyla's shoulder.

Then Tag looked up. "We haven't searched *everywhere*."

CHAPTER 14

INTO DANGER

Tag flew to the mouth of the volcano. Skyla and Blaze chased after him.

"You think it's in there?!" Skyla asked, peering over the ledge. Hot lava bubbles sizzled and popped inside.

"I'm going to fly down into the volcano," Tag said, taking off his armor.

Skyla's eyes went wide. "Tag! You can't go in there!"

"Peep!" Blaze cried. "Peep peep peep!"

Tag patted Blaze's head. "It's our last chance," he said as he stepped up to the ledge.

Tag flew down into the volcano, his tummy flip-flopping. He felt so hot he might melt. He looked along the walls for the purple stone. *The Ember Stone must be here somewhere!* Tag thought. He flapped to and fro, moving as close as he dared to the volcano's red-hot edges. *I can't stay in here much longer.*

Then he saw something at the very bottom of the volcano, on a small rocky ledge.

"I think I see it!" he called up to his friends. His heart beat as fast as his wings.

But as Tag flapped closer, a big lava bubble popped below.

"Ow!" he cried, as hot lava splashed his wing.

Tag flew up out of the volcano and landed beside his friends. "It's no good," he said. "I can't reach the ledge."

"I'm a great climber. Maybe I can climb down?" Skyla replied.

Tag nodded. "Just be sure to move fast—those walls are hot!"

Skyla scurried down into the volcano, gripping the rocky wall with her claws.

She got near the bottom, but slipped. The tip of her tail dipped into the lava. "Ow!" Skyla cried, scrambling out of the volcano.

"Are you okay?" Tag asked, as Skyla landed safely on the ground.

"I think so," Skyla said.

As Tag examined Skyla's tail, Blaze hopped onto the ledge. She leaned to look inside, then glanced back.

"Peep!" she called.

Tag and Skyla turned just as Blaze leaned too far forward. The firehawk fell down, down, down into the volcano.

"Blaze!" Tag flew after her. He looked and looked.

"I can't see her anywhere!" Tag said.

"This is all my fault!" Skyla cried.

Tag shook his head. "We *both* should have been watching her. We promised Grey we'd keep her safe."

Suddenly there was a loud **SCREEECH!** Blaze flew out of the smoky volcano with flaming wings. She was holding something in her beak!

"Blaze!" Tag cheered. "Blaze has the Ember Stone!"

CHAPTER 15

THE EMBER STONE

Blaze dropped to the ground. She was covered in ash.

Skyla brushed Blaze off. "I'm so glad you're okay!" she said, hugging Blaze. "*How* are you okay?"

"Blaze's feathers must have protected her," Tag said. He fed Blaze sips of water from the water pouch. "Remember what Grey told us—her feathers are stronger than any armor. Besides, firehawks are born in flame. I guess lava can't hurt her."

"That's why only a firehawk could find the Ember Stone—it was hidden inside a fiery volcano!" Skyla said.

Blaze gave a little peep and smiled.

"And it turns out you *can* fly!" Tag said.

Tag and Skyla crowded around to examine the Ember Stone.

Skyla squinted. “It’s smaller than I thought it would be.”

“Yes,” agreed Tag, remembering the rock paintings. “This stone is small with sharp, jagged edges. But the Ember Stone in the painting was large and round.”

"Thaddeus knew the firehawks. Maybe he knows something about the Ember Stone, too?" Skyla suggested.

The three friends rushed to the shoreline.

"Thaddeus!" Tag called across the water.

Blaze joined in. "Peeeep! Peee-eeep!"

"There he is!" cried Skyla, jumping up and down.

A large green head rose from the water. "Hullo," the old turtle said.

"We're hoping you might know something about this." Tag held up the Ember Stone. "Have you seen it before?"

Thaddeus scrunched up his eyes. He stared at the stone for a long time.

"The Ember Stone," Thaddeus said, finally. "The firehawks wanted to keep it hidden from Thorn. They tried to destroy it so that he couldn't use its powerful magic. But the stone could not be destroyed. Instead, it broke into pieces. The firehawks hid the pieces far and wide, so that Thorn would never find them."

“That’s why this stone is so small,” Skyla said. “It’s just *one piece* of the Ember Stone!”

“How many pieces are there?” Tag asked Thaddeus.

“The only animal who might know that is a firehawk,” Thaddeus said.

Tag, Skyla, and Thaddeus all looked at Blaze.

RETURN OF THE FIREHAWK

"I wish Blaze could speak," Tag said as they all sat on the beach with Thaddeus. "I'm sure she'd tell us what to do."

"Peep!" Blaze replied.

"This firehawk is still young," Thaddeus said. "She will speak soon enough."

"We should head back to Valor Wood," said Skyla. "Grey will know what to do next."

Tag shook his head. "I can't let Grey down now. I'll never become an Owl of Valor."

"We may not have found the *whole* Ember Stone, but we did find part of it," Skyla said, putting a paw on his wing. "That's got to count for something."

"This piece is powerless without all the other pieces," Thaddeus told them.

"Peep!" Blaze nudged Tag with her beak.

Skyla jumped up. "That's it! We'll search for the other pieces!"

"But we don't know where they are," Tag said as he pulled out Grey's map.

Skyla unrolled it on the sand, but the wind kept blowing it away.

"Here, use this." Tag placed the piece of Ember Stone onto the map to hold it in place.

Suddenly, the map glowed, brighter and brighter. It was so bright Tag had to cover his eyes with his wings.

When Tag looked again, a small shining dot appeared on the map. Far away from Fire Island.

Blaze tapped the dot with her beak.

Tag took a closer look. He hugged Blaze. "Grey said the map would show us the way." Tag pointed at the dot. "That must be where the next piece of the Ember Stone is!"

Skyla peered at the map. "This is going to be a *long* journey."

The three friends all gathered their belongings.

"I can take you to Blue Bay at the edge of the Shadowlands," offered Thaddeus.

Tag, Skyla, and Blaze climbed onto Thaddeus's back.

"Thank you for your help," Skyla said.

Thaddeus took them to shore.

"Peep!" said Blaze.

"Be careful," Thaddeus warned. "Thorn grows stronger every day. He will stop at nothing to find the pieces of the Ember Stone." He swam away.

Tag turned to his friends. "We don't have much time," he said. "Thorn's army will catch up with us soon."

"So," Skyla asked. "Where to next?"

"North," Tag told her with a smile. "To the Crystal Caverns."

ABOUT THE AUTHOR

KATRINA CHARMAN has wanted to be a children's book writer ever since she was eleven, when her teacher asked her class to write an epilogue to Roald Dahl's *Matilda*. Katrina's teacher thought her writing was good enough to send to Roald Dahl himself! Sadly, she never got a reply, but this experience ignited her love of reading and writing. Katrina lives in England with her husband and three daughters. The Last Firehawk is her first early chapter book series in the U.S.

ABOUT THE ILLUSTRATOR

JEREMY NORTON is an accomplished illustrator and artist who uses digital media to develop images and ideas on screen with light. He was an imaginative and prolific artist as a child, and he still tries to convey that same sense of wonder in his work. Jeremy lives in Spain. The Last Firehawk is his first early chapter book series with Scholastic.

The LAST FIREHAWK

The Ember Stone

Questions and Activities

1. Why does Tag want to become an Owl of Valor?

2. Why is protecting the firehawk an important job?

3. Reread the descriptions of the tiger bats (page 8) and the prickle ants (page 54). What do these creatures have in common with each other?

4. What happened to the other firehawks? Reread pages 61–62 if necessary.

5. How does Tag show that he is brave? Write an opinion paragraph about his bravest moment.